<u>HELLO, my name is Scott</u>
Wearing Nametags for a Friendlier Society

by Scott Ginsberg

HELLO, my name is Scott
Wearing Nametags for a Friendlier Society

Scott Ginsberg

Front Porch Publishing   2002

HELLO, my name is Scott
Wearing Nametags for a Friendlier Society
Copyright ©2002 by Scott Ginsberg
ISBN: 0-9726497-0-0

Library of Congress: 2002114698

Front Porch Publishing
2109 NW Irving
#103
Portland OR 97210

www.hellomynameisscott.com

A ship in harbor is safe, but that's not what ships are for.
—John Shedd

for Chelsea, who always made me smile

CONTENTS

Chapter 1

....

What's So Great about the Sidewalk?

Don't knock the weather. Without it, 90% of the people in the world wouldn't be able to start a conversation. —Kin Hubbard

The first time I drove down Route 27 I saw the most amazing house I had ever laid eyes on. The date was August 18, 1999, and I was about a half hour from completing my drive from St. Louis, Missouri to Oxford, Ohio. As I topped a large hill I saw a beautiful, wood two-story with a few acres of land and a pond in the back. That image permanently stuck in my mind. It looked like something out of a Thomas Kinkade painting, and it was simply breathtaking. About three seconds later, another image stuck in my mind: that of a blue truck traveling eighty miles an hour wildly honking at me: I had swerved into its lane while gazing at my dream house. So much for nostalgia.

Shortly after escaping death by stupidity, I thought back to my mental picture. It must have been the house's front porch that first attracted my attention. Ahhh, the front porch. I never had one growing up. I wish I had though—what a friendly gesture and welcoming symbol front porches represent. They extend a veritable invitation and an outlet for communication.

However, it seems that the front porch as a representation of hospitality is no longer a primary component of our daily lives. Throughout the last fifty years, dramatic sociological and technological changes have caused our lives to become more demanding, mobile, and individualistic than ever. Fortunately, we still get everything done. The only problem is that in our haste, we often isolate ourselves and sacrifice the friendly communications that once flourished in our society. In short, front porches don't seem necessary because people are either too busy or too scared to step onto them.

It simply boils down to a sociological problem that happens to be architecturally manifest. I've noticed that people's willingness to reach out and socialize with others has declined to a level that represents a bare minimum of only the required amount of interpersonal communication. It also seems that people are reluctant to communicate with strangers, and they allow this apprehension to get the best of them.

Essentially, people don't want to step onto someone else's front porch, and they don't want them stepping onto theirs. Here's a good example. Have you ever purposely looked off into the distance or stared at the pavement as you passed another person solely to avoid acknowledging them? People do this all the time. Or fixed your eyes on the floor lights when you enter the elevator? Ever notice that? I guess most people would rather brush up on their basic counting skills than talk to a stranger.

Not me.

Hello, my name is Scott.

To begin, I must first admit that I'm definitely not the most normal person in the world. But then again, who's to say what normal is, anyway? I suppose I'm just an eccentric, or in a broader sense, just an interesting guy. I am also by no means a genius or a literary scholar. At least, I don't think I am.

I am merely a man whose goal in life is to be friendly to everyone in order to break down walls of social trepidation, and spread the sheer joy that can be found through interpersonal interaction. To put it into better terms, I wish to invite everyone to sit on my front porch to help enhance our society's level of communication. And my individual method of accomplishing this goal is carried out by one simple, consistent act: **wearing a nametag.**

In the beginning, it all started out as an experiment. "What would happen if I wore a nametag *all the time*?" I wondered.

Maybe people would be friendlier.

Maybe people would say hello to me.

Maybe people would stare at me and think I was a complete weirdo!

I predicted that people's reactions to wearing a nametag would be pretty interesting. What I did not predict, however, was that wearing a nametag would eventually change my entire life.

So that's what this book is about—reactions. It's about stories of people stepping onto my front porch. It's about anecdotes and interesting predicaments in which I have found myself thanks to wearing a nametag, all for the sake of creating a friendlier society. Throughout these narratives, I will simply illustrate how I have serendipitously found wearing a nametag to be an effective means of stimulating friendly, interpersonal interactions with others, and how it has impacted me as well as my environment.

But I must preface by saying that this is not a self-help book, nor is it a "how to" book, nor am I trying to convince everyone to wear nametags. Let me repeat that: **I am not trying to convince everyone to wear nametags.** I'm realistic. I know that there's no way in hell everyone would want to wear nametags—it's just not gonna happen. Now, would it be great if everyone did wear nametags? Probably, but who really knows for sure?

HELLO, my name is Scott

The only thing I do know for sure is that by wearing a nametag, I have discovered my own simple, creative and unique way to encourage people to be friendlier and more sociable. If other people want to follow my lead and start wearing nametags, too, that's great! I won't stop them! But the key to changing a society to one of a more sociable and communicative nature is this: each person must find an appropriate mechanism through which his or her own personality can be effectively manifested.

The good news is that these mechanisms for increasing friendliness exist endlessly and can be used freely and abundantly by all who have the desire to create more front porches. I hope that someday you, too, will discover one that works for you.

Me, I choose to wear a nametag.

Welcome to my front porch.

Chapter 2

················

If You Wear it, They Will Come

Behold the turtle—he makes progress only
when he sticks his neck out. —James B. Conant

It was a Thursday in October 1999 during my sopho-more year of college at Miami University. My friend Nick and I had just finished attending a seminar on campus, after which we planned to meet some of our friends uptown for ice cream. The large group lecture we attended happened to require all its audience participants to wear nametags, so we decided on the way uptown to run an interesting experiment: both of us left our nametags on just to see what response we would get from other people.

We entered UDF, the local gas station/ice cream store to await the arrival of a few of our friends. This twen-ty-four-hour hangout was busy with customers and loitering students, so perhaps twenty or thirty people were standing around chitchatting.

Within about fifteen seconds of entering the store, Nick and I were bombarded with unexpected greetings and hellos from dozens of people, some of whom we didn't even know! Random people were striking up conversations, some were just saying hello to us, and some even shouted our names across the store!

"Nick! What's up dude!" or "Hey, Scott!" they would say.

There was nothing for us to do but cordially respond and talk to everyone, making new friends faster than we could handle! Throughout the night Nick and I each probably met twenty new people. We chatted with old friends and new strangers, all the while smiling at the success of our experiment.

About a year later Nick and I were reminiscing about how friendly everyone was that night. We thought it was great. And the best part about the whole situation was that we didn't even have to do anything! People willingly approached *us*, all because we left our nametags on.

After our conversation, I had an epiphany: maybe I should start wearing a nametag *all the time*. Pondering the ridiculousness of such an idea, I thought it would be better to simply run another, longer experiment. So I planned to test the effectiveness of wearing a nametag on people's willingness to be friendlier for an entire month. From the middle of October 2000 to Thanksgiving of 2000, I would wear a nametag all the time.

For about two weeks, the response was quite minimal. I later realized why people would initially say nothing to me. They thought I had just come from a convention or seminar in which nametags were required, or that I was working somewhere. It was also hypothesized by most, as I later found out from subsequent inquiries, that I just forgot to take my nametag off.

But after the first two weeks, something amazing happened. Every single day, between five and ten people, some strangers, some friends, would approach me to either say hello, and/or ask me why I was wearing a nametag. I quickly responded by either saying hello or explaining to them that it made people friendlier. Many people also asked me if I had just come from work or a convention.

When a month had gone by, hundreds of people knew why I was wearing the nametag. On a daily basis I met new friends and said hello to more people than ever before. Needless to say, I was astounded by the response. Furthermore, many fellow students from class proceeded to introduce themselves to me outside of class because they recognized "the guy with the nametag" so easily.

This made me realize that wearing a nametag also functioned as a great tool for helping other people remember my name. It turned out that mere acquaintances from class would become better friends with me because they took advantage of my nametag to strike up conversations that would have otherwise not existed.

It was just before Thanksgiving that I realized something: this was the greatest idea ever. I was amazed at how much friendlier and more willing to communicate people were, especially strangers. I also could see how much easier it was for other people to talk to me once they knew my name. Wow! What a simple way to create a friendlier society! I'm never taking this thing off!

HELLO, my name is Scott

Chapter 3

· · · · · · · · · · · · · · · · · ·

What's the Deal with Nametags?

Many of our fears are tissue paper thin, and a single, courageous step
would carry us clear through them. — Brendan Francis

So I never did take that thing off.

It has now been more than two years since I began
wearing a nametag, all day, every day. And, each of those
days are similar to the original day that started it all! During
these times of endless social interaction, I have consistently
observed and noted many evolutions in the phenomenon of
friendliness. First, I have become accustomed to explaining
why I am wearing a nametag all the time. For a while I had
quite a drawn out explanation, or as my friend Wade called it
"the nametag dissertation." This consisted of a rant about
societal friendliness, icebreakers, remembering names, talking to strangers, etc. However, since it took about a minute to
clarify everything, I felt it was not efficient.

After a few months I gathered the main points of my
theory and organized them into, what I like to call, "The Old
13er." I named it this because it took about thirteen seconds
to explain. It went something like this:

"I wear a nametag because it makes people friendlier and
more sociable and it helps them remember my name; and for
the people who don't remember my name, a quick and easy
visual stimulus such as a nametag eliminates their insecurity;
furthermore, psychologists say that the number-one word
people like to hear is their own name, so I get to hear my

name more, introduce myself to new people, they hear their name more, thus creating a friendlier society."

Yeah, it was quite a mouthful. In the beginning, many strangers to whom I explained my theory were shocked at the number of words that came out of my mouth in thirteen seconds. It was actually quite amazing. But alas, such a brilliant explanation was too complex and too wordy to repeat five times a day.

Well, that, and it scared some people.

So, since I didn't want to freak people out, I felt trimming The Old 13er down a bit would be more effective and efficient. The further evolution of my theory was complete in early 2001 when I began saying the "Skin and Bones" explanation:

"It makes people friendlier and more sociable and also helps them remember my name."

Simple.

Quick.

Perfect.

Now that you know what I say to people when they ask about my nametag, you may be wondering what people say to me. I have developed the following list of the most common reactions or comments made by people about my nametag. My memory for these conversations is quite accurate because of the frequency with which I have had the same conversation. Because most of these responses are so monotonous, I can recall almost every major category.

Q: Do you know you're still wearing a nametag?
A: Yes. I always wear it— (Skin and Bones).

As I have said, people often think there is a normal reason for wearing a nametag, such as employment or a seminar, which is why they ask this question. They're just waiting for me to exclaim, "Oh damn! I left this stupid thing on! I better peel it off!" Not bloody likely. Once I tell them the real reason, I usually get an eyebrow raise or a head nod since the explanation is so quick and easy to understand. Either that or they look at me like I'm crazy.

Q: Hey, Scott! Or, you must be Scott, right?
A: Hey! How are you? Or, yep, that would be me.

This would be a standard response to anyone who said hello to me, even if I weren't wearing a nametag. The only difference is that, in this case, those who say hello think they are witty and clever, since, "Scott has a nametag on and calling his name is really funny." It's actually quite remarkable how many hundreds of people have had the same facial expression and inflection in their voice when they say hello to me. In all honesty, I will be the first to admit that the joke is kind of funny if you're not aware of the reason I am wearing the nametag.

Although situations when this response occurs are often comical in nature, the scientific truth is that many people are merely taking advantage of the free offering of my name and using it to prompt their greeting to me. **This has**

proven to be the number one reason that strangers will talk to me because I am wearing a nametag. Essentially what people are doing when they say, "Hey, Scott," "You must be Scott, right?" or any other time they use my name in an inquiry is testing the waters. They are curious if that is my real name, or if I just wore a nametag for the hell of it. They desire to receive feedback from me and want to discover how I react to their greeting. So, when I respond back with a friendly "Hello" or "Hey, what's happening?" they are excited that their test was successful and that they received positive feedback from a stranger.

Q: Why are you wearing a nametag?
A: Skin and Bones.

Q: Do you always wear a nametag?
A: Yes. I never take it off— (Skin and Bones).

This inquiry is often followed with questions regarding the consistency of the nametag's appearance. For instance, it is often asked if I wear it when I go out at night, when I'm at home, or when I have job interviews. The answer: "For sure."

Q: Every time I see you, you have that nametag on!
A: That's right. I always wear it— (Skin and Bones).

Q: You know you can take off your nametag now.
A: No, I think I'm gonna leave it on. You see, I always wear it— (Skin and Bones).

This is, without a doubt, my favorite of all comments

What's the Deal with Nametags?

made to me, mainly because people feel they have the right to tell me what I can and cannot wear, which I find funny. Yes, it does frustrate me from time to time, but I get over it quickly. I suppose the reason people tell me that it's ok if I take off the nametag is because they assume I left it on from some prior occasion. This logic is completely expected and normal, so I don't hold it against them. But don't get me wrong, there have been times when I would love to respond with, "Hey, thanks. You know what, while I'm taking off my nametag, maybe I'll take off my pants too so you can kiss my hairy ass." But of course, that would be inconsistent with my friendly philosophy.

> Q: Do you work at the mall?
> A: No— (Skin and Bones).

This is only asked at the food courts in the malls. The reason for this inquiry is because mall employees receive discounts at the restaurants, and since I am wearing a nametag, it is logical to assume I am on my lunch break.

I know what you're probably thinking: "Have you ever said you worked at the mall to get discounted food?"

Well, that brings up an interesting moral question. But I cannot say I have ever tried it. I mean, as important as it is to save $1.49 on my Chick-Fil-A sandwich, I don't think I have the juevos to pull such a stunt. I suppose that in addition to friendly, charming, and sociable, I shall add honesty to my arsenal of personality characteristics.

HELLO, my name is Scott

Q: Where are you coming from that you need a nametag?
A: Nowhere, I just wear one all the time — (Skin and Bones).

Q: Is that so you don't forget your name?
A: No, it's not for me; it's for other people— (Skin and Bones).

I love this one. This supposedly clever remark usually comes from older people. In fact, it's very amusing to note the consistency of this joke from people over the age of forty. And, it always makes me smile every time I hear it. I guess they don't really think I can't remember my own name; it's just a certain type of humor used by a certain type of people.

Q: Do you watch a lot of Seinfeld?
A: Absolutely. Seinfeld is and always will be the greatest television show in the history of the world—but no, that's not where I got the idea to wear a nametag.

The only people who ask this question are the true, die-hard Seinfeld fans who recall an episode that involved nametags. In one show, Elaine suggested to her boyfriend an idea of requiring the entire city of New York to wear nametags in order to make people friendlier. As her boyfriend was an assistant to the mayor-elect, he recommended it to the mayor as a possible platform component. Subsequently, it resulted in his loss of the election by a landslide for what the news called "The Nametag Fiasco." However, I make sure to inform people that my initial reason for wearing a nametag did not spring from that episode. No matter how much I look

What's the Deal with Nametags?

like Kramer.

Q: Do you wear a nametag wherever you go, all the time?
A: Yep—all day, every day.

Q: Do you still wear your nametag if you're not wearing a shirt?
A: Oh, come on…what do you think I'm going to do,
stick a nametag on my bare chest? You better believe it.

Q: Hey, Scott, can you spare some change for a
homeless war veteran?
A: No.

Q: Hey…what's your name again? (pointing at my
nametag)
A: Scott. (Sometimes I answer with "Jack" or
"Marty" to play along.)

People seriously think they're clever with this remark.
The individuals who make this insanely obvious joke are often
the same ones who like to purposely call me another name in
order to be ironic. Hilarious.

Q: So, I guess you wear that nametag so everyone will
know who you are, right?
A: No, that's not the reason— (Skin and Bones).

In the multitude of explanations of my nametag theory,
this has been the most common misconception. It is true that
hundreds upon hundreds of people know me solely because of

my nametag, whether we're great friends or just acquaintances. It is true that nobody will ever forget my name. It is also true that I am approached by more strangers on a random day than anyone else I know.

It is *not* true, however, that I am wearing a nametag for the purpose of popularity. I can easily see how this conclusion could be made, since so many people know me solely as a result of my nametag. Similarly, I have also heard, "So...you're just doing this as an ego trip" or "You want everyone to know your name" many times over.

I must correct this erroneous assumption. Sure, I have become substantially better known in the past two years as a result of the nametag. Let the truth be known, during college I made so many friends that I almost couldn't keep up! But these friendships were all positive, serendipitous ramifications of wearing the nametag. Sure, having dozens of friends was a great asset, but that is not as important as the manner in which those friendships were formed, nor were they as important as the friendlier society of which they are a part.

However, I could understand how the *perception* may be that of a selfish desire to make everyone know me and have a thousand friends to boost my self-esteem, but the truth is the exact opposite. I am not doing this for me. I am doing this for every person in the entire world *except* myself. I am merely making others more sociable thus contributing to my dream of creating a friendlier society. The interactions created through my nametag are my own individual way to help enhance the level of communication in a society where face-to-face interaction is overshadowed and undervalued. So I am offering people lemonade to drink and a comfortable rocking chair to sit on, while relaxing on my front porch so

What's the Deal with Nametags?

we can be friends.

> Q: Do you ever feel that wearing a nametag eliminates anonymity for yourself?
> A: Yes, I do. And to tell you the truth, I don't care. I would gladly sacrifice a certain amount of privacy if it means other people are being friendlier.

After being asked this question a few dozen times, I came to the understanding that there is a very high percentage of people who would absolutely, never in their lives want to wear a nametag all the time. That's perfectly fine—wearing a nametag isn't for everybody. Truthfully, there have been times when I have attracted an undesirable element whose attention I was sorry to have gained. On the other hand, I've met some pretty interesting people and some really good-looking girls, too; wearing a nametag can be a bit of numbers game.

> Q: How long do you plan on wearing the nametag?
> A: Forever. (Let this statement be my declaration to my unborn children to bury my body with a nametag on it or I will come back from the dead to wreak havoc on their souls!)

&-&-&-&-&-&

You may remember that at the beginning of this book I explained the origin of my nametag. The reason I had it on in the first place was because I had previously attended a seminar that required me to wear it for the purpose of making introductions simpler and friendlier. So truthfully, I'm not the first person in history to wear a nametag to ease and expedite communication. Seminars, conventions, meetings, reunions, tours, and businesses have been using them for dozens of years for the same reason!

This is probably why most of the responses I have discussed are whether or not I have just come from some function that required me to wear a nametag. I suppose to most people that particular circumstance seems like the only reason some guy would be walking around with his name on his shirt.

However, I have chosen to wear a nametag in a different, more social context. Initially I just thought it would be fun to wear a nametag because I knew it made people more willing to say hello. But what I have found over the years is that wearing a nametag leads to more social "encounters" because it provides people with the one piece of information they need to take that pivotal first step to initiate a conversation with me: **my name.**

Knowing another person's name is extremely important in conversation, for it overcomes the natural barriers that separate strangers. This is because **a person's name is the ticket to beginning a conversation with him.** The likelihood of starting a conversation with someone whose name you *do* know will typically be higher than the likelihood of starting a conversation with someone whose name you *do not* know.

That's why I've met so many people and made so many friends by wearing a nametag—I have freely given them a golden opportunity to start a conversation and eventually become friends with me! It's the greatest ice breaker ever!

What's the Deal with Nametags?

In all honesty, what do these strangers *really* have to lose by talking to me anyway? They see my nametag as a perfect chance to start a conversation with a completely random person! My nametag provides the information that assures them of my approachability and their likelihood of getting a response!

And, they *always* get a response from me.

When I consistently reply with a kind greeting and a smiling face to their "test the waters" approach to friendliness, they are pleasantly surprised. Deep down they greatly appreciate my response because, whether or not they realize it, they have just said hello to a total stranger (or mere acquaintance) and it made them feel good. They felt good because I returned their friendly greeting, and that made them feel appreciated.

I have also noticed that once my returned greeting is accepted by strangers, they are willing to introduce themselves to me. This is a great advantage in conversations with new people because the longer you wait to give your name, the more uncomfortable you will become.

This reciprocal name exchange is an example of self disclosure, which is the act of making yourself manifest. The reason people are significantly more willing to give me their names as soon as we begin the conversation is because self disclosure is reciprocal respective to the level of intimacy that you have revealed. In short, when you tell someone something about yourself, e.g., your name, they will be likely to tell you that same thing about themselves.

In sum, my nametag functions as a front porch in the following way: when people see my nametag, they learn my name. Their knowledge of my name lowers their uncertainty about me as a stranger, and makes them feel less apprehensive about talking to me. Once that uncertainty is lowered, there is an increased probability for an encounter between us because I become more approachable to them. Finally, once they initiate a conversation with me and eventually reciprocate the offering of names, there is a better chance for new friendships to form.

Either that, or people are just screwing with me.

Chapter 4

·················

Nametag es Máquina

Order and simplification are the first steps
towards the mastery of a subject.—Thomas Mann

People often suggest that I change my way of nametagging. Here are the most common recommendations:

1. *Why don't you use the nametags that say, "HI, my name is...?"*

I have found that the simpler my nametag the more likely people will be to wonder why I'm wearing it. For instance, if the nametag said, "HI, my name is Scott" on it, the average passerby will be more likely to think I just came from a convention than if it were blank. I'm not saying that wearing those nametags for the same reason I do is wrong or substantially less effective; I just feel that in this case, simpler is better.

2. *Why don't you get one gold plated, nice nametag that you wear every day?*

I avoid these for the same reason since it may appear to be more normal to have such a nametag left on from a job such as clerk or tour guide. However, for those who know me well, normal is not one of my strong suits. So there goes that idea.

3. *Have you ever thought of changing the name every once in a while just to see if people notice?*

HELLO, my name is Scott

Yes, I have—and I tell about it in chapter six.

These responses, comments and questions about the manner in which I wear the nametag revolve around my **"Nametag Holy Trinity"** succinctly stated below:

SIMPLICTY

CONSISTENCY

REPETITION

■   **Simplicity:** My nametag is not flashy, wordy, or bright because its   purity   stimulates intrigue.

■   **Consistency:** The nametag always looks and is located the same exact way so it will be recognized and remembered.

■   **Repetition:** My nametag is worn all day, every day, with no exceptions. This increases willingness to communicate for people who don't say anything the *first* time they see me. Together with the idea of "consistency," repetition encourages people to step onto my front porch.

Also, the kind of nametag I use and the way my name is written is consistent. I ordered a few thousand from Maco, Inc. around October 2001 and those have become the standard form. Each tag is white with a red border with my name written as "Scott" in blue writing. I chose red and blue

Nametag es Máquina

because they are not too bold, but they still stand out. I would not want to write my name in yellow or orange, for instance, as the visibility and slight subtlety in my nametag important.

My physical characteristics also play an important role in the effectiveness of my nametag. When you see me walk by, I am about six-foot two (six-foot three with the hair), so for the majority of the people I know, my nametag rests at eye-level. This location provides an easy viewing position for oncoming pedestrians. Furthermore, I have strategically placed the nametag on my left breast, where it then becomes the *right* breast to the oncoming person. Since our society keeps to the right when approaching others, this leads to the increased probability of the nametag being noticed. People can easily see it as I'm approaching them, at which point they wonder why it's there. They then approach me, strike up a conversation and turn my empty front porch into an all-out party!

Many people have questioned the chest placement of my nametag. I'm sure it really doesn't make that much difference, but like every other aspect of wearing nametags, I have a theory for this, too. Employees or people attending seminars that are required to wear nametags will often be instructed to place them on their right breast. The reasoning behind this is that your nametag will be in the same line of sight as the handshake of a colleague, co-worker, or customer.

I completely agree with this method.

However, if you're shaking hands with someone, they've obviously *already decided* to come and talk to you. In this case, wearing the nametag on the *right* breast would make sense—but that's not why I wear a nametag. My goal is to bring from a larger proximity people who *have not already decided* to talk to me. If you see someone walking ten feet ahead of you, it makes more sense to have the nametag in a location that will be the most accessible from their "right side of the road" vantage point.

There are a few other wearing specifics. The first is the availability issue. I keep a consistent stock of a few thousand pre-made, exact-same nametags. I usually grab one each day, or whenever one is needed. For instance, I may just leave a nametag on a shirt if I only wear it once and don't plan on doing laundry.

Having such a large inventory may sound outrageous and a bit obsessive-compulsive. Well, it is, but that's just the way I am. But as I explained in the Holy Trinity, consistency is of the utmost importance. This particular issue also comes into play when the weather gets cold. So, if I wear a coat I will have two nametags on, since the coat will cover up the one on my shirt.

Consistency is also important in situations that may even seem ridiculous. I always keep one on my shirt, even if I am just sitting around in my apartment. I know it sounds excessive, but you never know whom you might run into taking out the garbage.

Another key wearing specific is having extra nametags. There will always be situations when a new one will be needed; for example, stormy weather or my own sloppy eating habits.

And of course, when people rip it off.

This brings me to an interesting point. Since I always wear a nametag all day, every day, many pseudo-comedians think it would be humorous to rip off my nametag. The thought is, "You always wear that damn thing, and I am going to rip it off and make me responsible for your *not* wearing a nametag. Ha ha!"

I played chess once in my life with my good friend Pete and he kicked my ass. But I did learn a valuable lesson about staying six moves ahead of your opponent. This strategy resulted in my carrying a few extra nametags in my wallet, car, and bags. Should a clever person pull off my nametag and rip it up in triumphant victory, I laugh and whip out another one and stick it on my shirt before the original torn tag hits the floor.

If you've never witnessed this act, it surely is a thing of beauty. The first time it happened to me was at the end of my junior year of college. I was at a bar with my friend Kristin when her friend Angela, whom I really had a crush on at the time, thought it would be funny to rip my nametag off. Sure enough, she peeled it off and I watched the pieces trickle to the beer soaked floor as she laughed gleefully. I casually smiled and pulled out my wallet, took another one out and stuck it on. She couldn't believe it! She almost fell to the floor laughing. It was priceless. I should have asked her out on a date right then and there—she probably would have said yes.

In addition to the physical characteristics of the nametag itself, there are also some personality traits I possess that add to the success of my using my nametag as a front porch. Most importantly, I am quite an articulate individual. After almost four years as a disc jockey and ten years as a musical performing artist, I have developed a pleasant, conversational voice for myself. This does wonders for my explanations.

Furthermore, I am a very genuine, outgoing guy whose appearance doesn't repel people. Interpersonally, people are attracted to other people for a variety of reasons, but in my case, the overriding one is my likeability and the fact that I am easy to talk to. All of these qualities combined with a handsome smile and animated hand gestures allow strangers to perceive me as a friendly and approachable person. Modest too, obviously.

Chapter 5

·················

A Teacher Called by Any Other Name is Still a Teacher

Humor is by far the most significant activity
of the human brain. — Edward DeBono

Most of my professors in college were aware of my nametag, but they usually didn't say anything about it. I guess they just assumed I wore it for my job or some other function during the day, and since they only saw me for a short while, they didn't realize that it was on all the time.

But the first day of Marketing 431—Logistics Management—I had no idea what I was in for. Someone had recommended the course to me because the teacher was supposed to be great and the class equally great. Talk about an understatement.

If I ever learned my lesson about tardiness, it was from Dr. Tom Speh. The second day of class I arrived about ten minutes late and I paid for that mistake the entire semester.

Stupid snooze button.

I sat down at ten minutes past the hour with thirty of my peers and one drill-sergeant teacher staring at me. "You must be Ginsberg."

"Yes sir," I said as I sank into my chair.

"Do you know you still have your nametag on?"

"Yeah, I always wear it. It makes people friendlier and more sociable and helps them remember my name."

"Really?" he asked.

"Yeah."

"So you wear it all the time?"

"Yep."

"That's a great idea," he chuckled (as did the whole class). At this point in my year-long sporting of the old nametag, I was used to classmates eventually saying a word or two to me. What I was not used to was the professor starting each lecture with some joke/comment about my nametag to the entire class. Being the reciprocal jokester that I was, I did my best to remain calm and cool and responded twice weekly to such Dr. Speh comments as:

"It's good to see you still have on your nametag."

"Morning, Scott. You see, I still remember your name because of that nametag."

"It looks like you have two on today...one for your jacket and one for your t-shirt. That's good thinking."

"That's Scott over there."

It never ended.

It wasn't until a few weeks into the semester that Dr. Speh's daily inquiry about my nametag began to involve the whole class. He suggested that I bring nametags for the entire class. I said, "Sure, I got thousands of them."

The following day Dr. Speh continued to mock my brilliant idea by wearing his own gold plated Miami University nametag. His was a bit fancier than mine, but of course I never received Teacher of Century like the great Tom Speh did.

A week or two later, when my new shipment came in the mail, I left out a hundred blank ones during the three hours I spent one Saturday night filling out 1500 standards. These were to be brought to class the following Tuesday and dispersed to my classmates.

I walked into class on Tuesday about five minutes early

A Teacher Called by Any Other Name is Still a Teacher

and set the nametags on the front desk, just waiting for Speh to notice them. He walked in at 11:02, his usual slightly tardy arrival, and put his books down before he noticed a 100-pack of familiar red and white stickers staring at him.

He looked up and smiled. "Well, class, Scott has been nice enough to bring nametags for everyone, so I'm going to pass these out now and I would like you all to put one on."

Just about every single person in the class sneered back at me in irritated amazement as if to say, "Are you kidding me? Is this moron seriously making us all wear these stupid nametags?"

Yes. Yes, he is.

All the students received one and put them on their shirts, shaking their heads during the writing and sticking process, still looking back and smiling at me. Dr. Speh even put one of my donated nametags on, although it didn't read "Tom."

He decided to write "Richie" on his nametag. A girl in the front asked why he wrote Richie, and he said, "I always wanted to be called Richie." Fair enough, I suppose.

At 12:15 on the dot, the standard closing time for Marketing 431, thirty students rested our writing hands and sighed in relief as another grueling day of Logistics ended. On my way out the door, Speh flipped to me the half-used pack of nametags and thanked me. I immediately flipped them back to him and said, "Keep 'em for another time." He smiled back and I walked out.

The next day at 11:02, Speh walked in with another nametag on, although this time it read "Elwood." By this time in the semester, our class was used to his silly classroom antics, so nobody said anything to Professor Blues Brother. I, of course, noted the name down in my 431 note book, thinking there was a method to his madness.

As it turned out, there was no method to his madness. He was just screwin' with me.

He's a funny guy if you ever get a chance to make it over to the Miami University Marketing Department. Any of his fellow professors or past students will tell you so. In addition to crazy jokes and returned-product stories in class, he also managed to pick out people each day to make fun of. Most days it was me.

About a week after the Akroyd incident, Speh walked into class with yet *another* one of my nametags on. This time it read something a bit more obscure: Norb. In fact, I've never actually met a "Norb." I had a counselor at camp when I was ten who was named "Norm," but never a Norb. Is that even a real name?

I'm sure Norb is a real name, and there are probably many fine people out there with that particular name. However, I think Norb was chosen by Dr. Speh since it seemed like the most random and unheard of name possible. This helped him mock my nametag phenomenon to its fullest.

Let the truth be known, Speh can mock me all he wants (and he does), but the following testimonial from Justin D. Ellis, former classmate and friend, will provide new light from another perspective on the subject:

"After that class with Speh, my friend Jeff and I went to lunch. I kept my nametag on. There were quite a few people in the cafeteria, and every time I would pass one of them, they would look at my nametag. However, nobody said anything to me—at least, not yet. After eating and resting at home for a bit between classes, I headed outside to take the yellow route to class. The bus stop is where it all happened. Every Tuesday and Thursday at the same time, I would go out there and wait with this one girl. I knew she lived right across from me because I saw her walk out of her apartment around the same time as me, but we never said anything to each other. Usually, we would both just stare at the ground and not say anything, but this day was different—I had my nametag on. She kept looking over at me with a strange face until about a minute went by and our eyes met. I looked at her and she said, "Hi, I'm Sarah. I live across from you." I then introduced myself and we talked until the bus came. We talked on the bus ride and all the way to Upham Hall, where we both had class. For the rest of the year, we spoke all the time and Sarah became my new friend. Those nametags were miracle workers."

Dr. Tom Speh had the following words to contribute:

S-C-O-T-T, white name tag, blue lettering, red border. It was day one of Logistics Management class, and there was the kid— first row, last seat, with the guinea pig hairdo (large clumps of hair going in random directions) with this nametag emblazoned over his heart.

So, what is in a name (tag), that is? A very interesting person, indeed.

I thought to myself as I scanned this new group of logistics neophytes, "Did this kid just come from some fraternity function? A social event? A seminar class where everyone wears name tags? Or was he just plain weird?" It was hard to focus on the rest of the students with this guinea pig hairdo kid wearing S-C-O-T-T on his chest sticking out like a sore thumb. Being a joker by trade and never wanting to miss an opportunity for levity and humor, I couldn't resist inquiring, "What's with the nametag?"

The dead pan response from Scott in the back with the hair, "I always wear it—it makes people friendlier and more sociable. Yeah, I've met a lot of people this way and it helps them remember me, too."

My first thought, which of course I had to blurt out, "Don't they think you are strange?"

The nametag kid responded, "Yeah, most people do, but you won't believe all the new friends I've met."

Then, the thought of all students wearing nametags was mortifying to me. One of my great in-class performances is to name all the students and their hometowns by the third day of class. It is challenging, but a terrific way to get to know the students, and the theatrical appeal is great as I go around the room methodically naming each student and the place from which they hail. My God, nametags would forever eliminate one of the basic foundations upon which my rather daunting reputation had become established!

As I always do, I selected a limited number of students to chide, cajole, and harass during the course of the semester. This select group is usually made up of those students who are somehow interesting and different, and who, importantly, have thick skins. Mr. Nametag was just too enticing to pass up. There were no shortages of opportunities to inquire about the daily and often unusual experiences brought on by the nametag.

One cold day, a marvelous opportunity presented itself, which just couldn't go unrecognized—"DOUBLE

A Teacher Called by Any Other Name is Still a Teacher

TAGGING." This event let us move to a significantly higher level with the funny business associated with the name tags. Scott arrived at class in a long, black, heavy winter coat. Clearly pasted to the left breast of the winter coat was the all-too-familiar S-C-O-T-T, with the red border and white background. Upon removing the coat, lo and behold, a second S-C-O-T-T on Mr. Meet and Greet's shirt. There was no way that Scott would go unrecognized in any kind of weather, whether he was seen in the warm confines of the classroom or the blustery elements outside.

I even had a chance to emulate the nametag kid when he handed me a surplus ration of nametags from his vast inventory of the red and white rectangles. It was great fun to arrive in class each day with a nametag bearing a different moniker each time—Richie, Norb, Elwood. Each day the anticipation from the class was building to see who would be teaching that day, and it also afforded the chance to pay homage to some very exotic, although obscure names.

Interestingly, it is not really the fun we had with the nametag distraction that stands out. What I came to learn from the whole process was that Scott was really an incredible person, with a real passion for life and a capacity to learn lessons far beyond the class material. Here was a person willing to be different, willing to stand out on a daily basis, willing to accept the derision that might be directed his way, yet a person who was absorbing the lessons of life that being different creates.

S-C-O-T-T: it's not the nametag; it's what's underneath that matters.

HELLO, my name is Scott

Dr. Norb Speh and I in the Miami University
School of Business in May 2002

Chatper 6
....
HELLO, My Name is Randy

You are what you pretend to be.
So be careful what you pretend to be. — *Kurt Vonnegut*

As I noted in chapter three, I am often asked if I ever change the name on my nametag. My response is always the same: "No, I always keep it the same for consistency."

Except for this one time...

The best part about Halloween is that girls can get away with wearing the most revealing and socially unacceptable clothing, accessories, and makeup without being labeled slutty. I love it. Some say it's the greatest holiday ever.

I've always had fun costumes myself, ranging from a ventriloquist dummy, to a dead guy, to a Ghostbuster. But I never came up with the one really clever costume that everyone talked about or noticed. I think one of the best costumes I ever saw was at a fraternity Halloween party. When I walked in the door I noticed that one of the brothers who was in charge of greeting people was covered in all gold paint. That was pretty much all he was covered in. I was shocked when I saw him saying hello to everyone, but still wondered what he was dressed up as. I had to ask, so I approached him and popped the question.

"I'm an Oscar."

It took about three seconds to realize he meant the award. Hilarious.

Boy, to walk around in October with no clothing on sure took some balls—and everyone at the party could see them.

HELLO, my name is Scott

I suppose such brilliant costumes have inspired me over the years, but I never dressed up with that same creative boldness. In 2001, I had initially planned to dress up as a Buddhist monk. Unfortunately, the robe I bought was way too tight, so maybe it wasn't the best choice after all.

Stupid body hair.

While pondering other possible costume ideas, I remembered a conversation I had with a friend earlier that week about my nametag. She asked if I ever considered changing the name to Bob or something, just to see if people noticed. I told her that I always wanted to do that, but never found a good time to do so.

I would simply change my nametag as my costume! But what name would I choose? If I wasn't going to be Scott, who would I be?

Not Bob. That name's too unoriginal and too obvious. I like the name Jack, but I don't think I look like a Jack. Greg? Jimmy? What about Andrew? Nah...I don't like any of those either.

But I have always loved the name Randy. I don't know why, I just think it's a great name. Whenever I tell jokes or stories that include fictitious characters, I tend to use the name Randy. I think it's a great name to say, and if you don't have a friend or relative named Randy, I would suggest you get one.

It was October 31, 2001. I had made the decision. I dug up one of my blank nametags and filled it out like no other nametag I had ever filled.

At 9:10 when I got out of the shower and finished getting dressed, the crucial time had come. I stuck the pseudo-nametag on my chest and looked at myself in the mirror.

HELLO, My Name is Randy

Randy. Today, I was Randy.

It looked weird. I felt violated. I felt...different.

Well, hell, I was different. I was Randy! Ha!

This was a rare day. Not only because I wore a different nametag, but also because I actually walked to class instead of taking the bus. I arrived at my Management lecture a little before 10:00 AM. I knew the key to successfully pulling off such a costume was silence and subtlety, so I was to act no different than ever before. Just let the people do the talking.

My friend Marna was the first to notice. She already was in her seat, so I walked by with a traditional, "Morning," to which she responded, "Hey, Scott. Oh, wait...you're *Randy* today?"

"Yep. This is my Halloween costume."

She chuckled at the cleverness of such a costume. I smiled back and realized what a great idea this was.

After class I took my usual stir-fry lunch over to WMSR Redhawk Radio, where I worked as Promotions Director. My friend Rob, the music director, was cataloging on the computer when I walked in. We chatted about the usual music-related stuff, ate our fortune cookies and I was back on my way to my 1:00 advertising class. He hadn't said anything about my change in identity, but he did look at me kind of strange.

I arrived at Marketing 441, Advertising and Promotions about 1:00. I sat down as usual, and nothing was said. When my professor Ellen Young arrived, we began class with some overhead notes. There was a picture about a particular advert that I wanted to comment on, so I raised my hand. Without hesitation, she pointed to me and said, "Yes, Randy."

I explained my point as she chuckled, but only a few other people realized what the joke was. After my comment, she said, "So, you're Randy today?" As with Dr. Speh, the entire class turned around to see what she was talking about. "It's my Halloween costume," I explained.

Everyone laughed.

Some time later I was called on again as "Randy." Sitting next to me my friend Laura looked at me strangely. She looked away and then took one of those slanted eye-brow double-takes at my nametag.

"Oh, wow, I didn't even notice that…uhh…Randy," she laughed.

After class was dismissed and the students were packing their bags, I heard the name Randy called by a familiar voice, although I didn't respond at first. Once I heard the name called again in what sounded like my general direction. I looked over at my friend Brandis who apparently had been calling my new name several times. I apologized for not responding since I wasn't used to being called Randy. From that point on I knew I would have to listen closely to what came out of other people's mouths on that Halloween.

After class I ventured over to the dining hall for some coffee. When I made my way to the checkout line the clerk said, "Don't you usually have a nametag that says 'Scott' on it?"

"Yeah, I just have this one on today as my Halloween costume."

"Huh! That's hilarious!"

This was great.

See! Consistency—one of the keys to pulling off the nametag. So, when you just *slightly change* that consistency, people will notice. The funniest part about that incident was that I didn't even know that checkout girl!

On the way to my final class of the day I heard a shout

that came from the back of the quad from a familiar female voice. "Hey, Randy!"

"Hey, Brandis!" I yelled back.

The people who played along really made it work. I went to a Halloween party later that night with my friends Dan and Farmer who also called me Randy. We went to a few bars and parties that night. Many of my friends who saw me greeted me as Scott, but when they got closer they noticed the nametag and started calling me Randy.

I still have that nametag to this day.

HELLO, my name is Scott

Chapter 7

·················

The Nametag that Wasn't There

When patterns are broken, new worlds can emerge.
— Tuli Kupferberg

My metamorphosis to Randy was a turning point in my experiences with wearing a nametag. That incident was the first time I used the existing recognition of my nametag as a means for a hilarious experiment/joke. However, it would not be the last.

Since my entire life is an experiment anyway, I figured I would document an official record of the most interesting experiment of all: *not wearing the nametag for an entire week.* The final week of classes of my senior year, April 22-28, 2002 would be the last known to man that the world would see Scott Ginsberg without a nametag.

There were a few reasons behind this terrifying act. First and foremost, I just wanted to screw with people. I figured that since everyone was so used to seeing my nametag, taking it off would be a great way to confuse them. I was also curious to note how many people noticed that I didn't have my nametag on. But more importantly, I wanted to compare the adverse effects in others' willingness to communicate.

Over a year and a half had gone by without the removal of my nametag. So this period of time proved to be more than sufficient as a basis to create its recognition, and I had a feeling the responses would be quite interesting.

Throughout this experiment, I kept a notebook with me to write down all that transpired. The first week included data I recorded about each person who noticed my nametag was gone. I wrote down their names, what they said, how they said it, and where they saw me.

In the attempts to keep my results accurate and without bias, I told no one that I was not going to wear a nametag for a whole week. Furthermore, at no time before, during, or after the experiment did I change any of my own behavior, actions, or communications— other than the nametag itself.

The first person to notice was my good friend Joe who exclaimed as we shook hands in front of a bike rack, "This is the first time in like two years that I haven't seen you wear a nametag."

"I know—I'm running an experiment to note the number of responses and the adverse effects in friendliness as a result of not wearing a nametag," I said. He laughed as I wrote his name down. He was excited to be the first person to notice.

Not surprisingly, the second person to notice and immediately yell at me was Dr. Tom Speh. "Where's your nametag? I'm gonna forget who you are," he joked. I told him about the experiment and he told me he was excited to hear the results.

Throughout the first week, fifty-eight people approached me and asked why I didn't have it on. I explained the reasoning to everyone and they were all quite amazed. The people who noticed can be categorized as follows:

58 total people
27 men
31 women
 3 professors
 2 strangers

The Nametag that Wasn't There

The most common reactions were:

> Where's your nametag?
> Not wearing the nametag today?
> This is the first time I have seen you without a nametag!
> Are you not wearing the nametag anymore?

Many were discombobulated, including me. I must admit it was one of the hardest things I have ever done. Which is pretty sad.

> I felt strange.
> I felt naked.
> I felt normal. Ugh! Gross!

Over the years the sole reason behind wearing a nametag has been, and always will be, to create a friendlier society through increased social interaction. I knew from experience that people were a lot more sociable and more willing to communicate, but I never had made a comparison between stranger interactions while wearing a nametag, and stranger reactions while not wearing a nametag.

Interestingly enough, during the first week without "Scott" plastered on my chest, I did not have one conversation with a stranger. I didn't have one friendly shout across the room from an unfamiliar person. At no point did mere acquaintances introduce themselves to me and begin conversations since they now knew my name and felt less apprehensive. I can't remember a retail clerk, card swiper, unknown-passerby, or waitress who cordially used my name in any of our discussions.

It really hurt me to take it off—not because I didn't get all the attention as usual, but because all this time I had been making people smile daily by increasing friendliness—and I had to stop that! It killed me! In fact, Thursday morning of that week I woke up in the middle of the night in a shivering cold sweat!

Not really.

On Monday of the second week, the nametag returned. It was good to have it back. Thank God, too, because so many of my shirts had these huge, dirty, sticky, rectangular marks on the chest area that looked pretty gross if they weren't covered by a nametag.

During this time, I continued to record data on people's reactions. The first observation was how many people responded to me about the nametag's return. Over the course of the week, thirteen people asked me or talked to me about the return of the nametag. Most people were glad to see it back on; however, some were confused. I explained again to all of them why I had run the experiment. Interestingly enough, each of the thirteen people in the second week who asked about the return of the nametag was also part of the group of fifty-eight people in the first week who questioned its original absence.

The second observation was the high number of friendly stranger interactions. "Stranger interactions" were verbal communications from strangers or people I hardly knew who used my nametag as an outlet for increased interpersonal communication; i.e., anything from chapter three. Amazingly, I recorded that twenty-five strangers approached and talked to me. Without the nametag, these encounters

The Nametag that Wasn't There

would not have occurred. To illustrate, these are samples of conversations from April 29 through May 5, 2002—and also good examples of daily, average interactions that I have all the time.

1.   Stir Fry Chef: Monday, 11:45 A.M.—When taking my order she said, "So Scott, would you like chicken or beef?" This student with the attractive smile had pretty much the same one-lined conversation with me that she had with all her customers, but after she cooked the dish, I made sure to glance at her nametag and say, "Thanks, Lauren." She smiled again.

2.   Bus Driver: Monday, 2:40 P.M—I boarded the Miami Metro to hear him say, "Good afternoon, Scott!" I replied with the same as we smiled to each other.

3.   Girls on Campus: Monday, 2:52 P.M.—As I walked to class two students I did not know both smiled and one of them said "Hey, Scott," to which I replied, "Afternoon, Ladies."

4.   Stranger at a Bar: Tuesday, 11:14 P.M.—While playing a video game with my friend Mike, a girl asked me why I was wearing a nametag. I explained it to her, and then she (my new friend Liz) and I talked for about ten minutes.

5.   Girls off Campus: Wednesday, 1:36 P.M.—I was returning home from lunch when two girls across the street sitting on their front lawn greeted me with, "What's up, Scott?" I waved back with yet another pleasant greeting.

6.   Stranger on the Street: Wednesday, 8:02 P.M.—As I stood in front of a restaurant waiting for a friend, a girl asked if my name was Scott, then introduced herself as Carrie. We talked for a short while.

7.   **Unknown Boyfriend:** Wednesday, 11:56 P.M.—Late one night outside another restaurant, I heard someone call my name, but I didn't know who he was. He explained that he was the boyfriend of a friend of mine, after which Pete and I finally became acquainted.

8.   **Friend of a Friend:** Thursday, 12:31 A.M.—As I stood outside of the same restaurant in #7, a friend of a friend introduced herself to me.

9.   **Friend of a Friend of a Friend:** Thursday, 12:32 A.M—After #8, a friend of a friend of a friend introduced herself to me as well.

10.   **Random Girl:** Thursday, 1:05 A.M.—As I walked down the street, a girl waiting in line to get into a bar said, "What's up, Scott?" I said, "I'm done with college, I feel great!" She explained that she was also done with college, so I gave her a high five and a smile and walked on.

11.   **Classmate:** Thursday, 1:58 A.M.—As I passed a table full of people, a classmate of mine to whom I never had been properly introduced called my name, and I went over to the table to be introduced to him and his friend.

12.   **Drunken Idiot:** Thursday, 2:09 A.M.—While waiting to meet some friends, a girl came up to me, or should I say

The Nametag that Wasn't There

stumbled up to me and said, "Hi, Scott, I'm Megan." She probably could have also introduced herself as "annoying, drunk girl who spilled her Long Island Iced Tea on my sandals."

13. **Mall Employee:** Friday, 1:47 P.M.—While waiting an eternity for my girlfriend to *try on, not purchase* six pairs of shoes, one of the salesman asked about my nametag and we chatted for a bit.

14. **Passerby at Bar:** Friday, 10:29 P.M.—On my way to the bathroom at a local bar, a guy who passed me greeted me with a friendly "Hey, Scott," to which I replied the same.

15—21. Random Strangers: Friday, 11:30 P.M. to 11:45 P.M.—I said hello to a variety of individuals from several larger groups while walking down the street.

22. **Mother of a Fellow Graduate:** Saturday, 3:38 P.M.—Clad in my cap and gown, I walked to the location of the ceremony; a mother driving her son to the same location said, "Congratulations, Scott!" I thanked her. I think this is one of my favorite stranger interactions in all the years I have been wearing my nametag.

23. **The Anti Nametag:** Saturday, 10:48 P.M.—I had a five-minute conversation with a girl who completely shot down my theory about nametags. I must say, for being intoxicated she really had a strong argument. I nodded and respected her position on the subject. After she was done I smiled and said, "You make great points and I appreciate your opinion, but whether or not you like my nametag you have just spent five minutes of your time talking to me because I was wearing it. That's fine that you don't like it, but you're doing exactly what I hoped would happen—increase friendly interaction with strangers." She didn't say much after that.

24.   Bouncer: Saturday, 11:24 P.M.—On the way out of the same bar where the Anti-Nametag was found, the bouncer at the door told the people crowding around to "Let Scott through." He smiled and it was a very nice gesture. I thanked him and smiled back.

25.   Couple on the Street: Saturday, 11:57 P.M.—A girl named Sally told me she had seen me for years with the nametag and wanted to introduce herself. She also introduced her boyfriend Wallace to me. We chatted for a few minutes and went our separate ways.

It was a good week.

Chapter 8

....

Some Folk'll Never Wear a Nametag,

and then Again Some Folk'll

I couldn't find an appropriate quotation to summarize this chapter.
— Scott Ginsberg

In two years it never occurred to me that *other people* would actually consider wearing a nametag and applying it to their own lives. Many friends have told me that they wanted to start wearing nametags as well, to which I always replied with supportive enthusiasm.

"You know what, Scott? I think I might start wearing a nametag, too! It's such a great idea!"

"Sweet, you should do it! It'd be great if you would help spread the message about friendliness!" I would say.

"Nah...I don't wanna steal your idea," is the common reply.

Well, I hate to tell ya, but it's not really my idea. Nametags have been around for many years and have been worn by millions of people. Just like them, I, too, want to encourage people to be friendlier. I simply choose to wear it all the time to make people friendlier all the time; or, at least, more often than not.

Some strangers ask me if I have any extra blank nametags to give to them, but, unfortunately, all my extras are pre-labeled. So it was to my surprise in the winter of 2000, a few months after my initial nametag experiment, that two other people decided to follow my lead.

And to think, this whole time I thought I was the only nut out there.

HELLO, my name is Scott

Upon my arrival in St. Louis for the Thanksgiving holiday, I realized that I had not yet told my family about my latest friendly endeavor. I became the subject of ridicule at our annual feast that Thursday night.

My brother told me I was a total moron, but he'd been calling me that my whole life so it really didn't make much difference. My parents merely shook their heads and chuckled at the idea. I suppose they had already come to terms with the fact that I was an idiot, so it wasn't bothersome.

But when I discussed the idea with two of my cousins, Collin and Justin, they thought it was a great idea. They asked what reactions people had and how it worked to make them friendlier. I told them everything, and after a few minutes they both asked if I minded their implementing my front porch labeling system.

"Absolutely not!"

I was so excited. I couldn't believe they were really going to do it! I knew that most people wouldn't seriously start wearing a nametag like I did, but they were pretty gung-ho. Even better, Collin and Justin were outgoing, friendly and individualistic people. So their adoption of wearing a nametag to make people friendlier was quite fitting for their personalities.

"Just tell everyone it makes people friendlier and more sociable and also helps them remember names," I instructed them.

They quickly memorized Skin and Bones. About a month later, Collin and Justin bought their own nametags so they, too, could begin spreading the message about a friendlier society.

I was eager to hear about some of the responses they got. Since our houses were only about eighty yards apart, it was easy to stay updated. Whenever the family got together, the three of us made sure to keep each other informed about the stories, jokes and conversations our nametags garnered.

I have asked Collin and Justin to provide some stories and perspective on wearing nametags. Trailing my streak by only a few months, the two of them have bravely created front porches of their own and helped contribute to the creation of a friendlier society in their own way.

Collin Diedrich

In the beginning I felt really weird, but I eventually got used to it. The idea was interesting to me, and it sounded like something that was right up my alley. Now, at this point after almost two years of wearing a nametag, it's weird if I don't have it on.

I had been wearing my nametag for about a month or so when I went on a college visit with some friends. I was still in high school at the time and was trying to decide on a school that would suit me. At a party I was confronted by this "surfer dude" who tried to give me a scare by loudly yelling, "Hey, Collin, what's up, man!"

Even though I had no idea who this guy was, we carried on a moronic conversation that tricked my friends into thinking that I really knew him. It was pretty funny.

But to tell you the truth I was not too fond of him because I think he made fun of my shoes. Oh, well. It doesn't matter because I got a chance to make a new friend and talk to someone who probably would have normally ignored me.

Now, whenever a stranger says, "Hi, Collin!" I immediately pick up on the friendliness and carry on a conversation. It's kind of redundant to me because I have had it about a hundred times, but I still enjoy it.

In the beginning, my friends at school came up to me and said things like:

1. "You can take your name tag off now."
2. "I am gonna steal your name tag."

To each of these, I responded with:

1. "I will only take my name tag off when society smiles."
2. "Touch my baby and I will kill you!"

In regard to the way I wear my nametag, I have always been consistently inconsistent. I always write my name on the tag differently, in a different font and with a different pen.

I also like to change where my name tag is located just for the hell of it. I guess I can understand Scott's idea of keeping the nametag consistent, but sometimes I just like to mess with people's heads.

Recently, I received a great shipment of custom nametags with a variety of colors and cartoon drawings on them. I have a total of seven different name tags, and I have worn them at least twenty times apiece. I do this to keep people on their toes. Here's a list of the different patterns I use:

1.   HELLO, I'm....

This one has confetti all over it. It's my personal favorite. Made for a party or some other fun activity.

Some Folk'll Never Wear a Nametag, and then Again Some Folk'll

2. Frogs

It's a cute one; I think it's designed for a pre-school class.

3. The Sun

You just can't go wrong with the sun.

4. Bright Colors

Around the edges there's a great rainbow of different colors.

5. HELLO, my name is...

Blue and Red. This one is the standard name tag used at most functions or conventions.

6. Blank

There is a red and blue border. This is another standard name tag often worn at a lot of functions.

7. HELLO

This one is the most boring nametag. It is on a marble background.

I actually turned a job down one summer because I was not allowed to wear a nametag while on the clock. That was a glorious day for me and the cause I stood for. Truthfully, even if they *had* let me wear my nametag, I probably wouldn't have taken the job because that place sucked anyway.

Much like Scott, my friends are constantly asking me to give them nametags to wear around for the day. I always have blank spares in my wallet so that is never a problem. It makes me so happy to give people nametags and it's really fun to have a bunch of people wearing them throughout the day. I must say days like those are the ones that keep me wanting to wear my nametag forever.

One of my favorite stories happened when I went to Italy for my senior trip in the spring of 2002. I didn't speak any Italian so communication was at a minimum throughout the week—that is, until the last night when I was in Rome.

I was talking to the owner of one of the coffee shops about which drink to choose because I couldn't figure out what the heck the menu meant. Since I was having a tough time ordering, it was taking forever.

Then he said, "Collin, be a man, get a double espresso."

He smiled and I agreed to get the drink he suggested. I paid and eventually drank the most bitter and repulsive drink that has ever touched my lips! It was horrible! To make matters worse, he insisted that I talk to him for about an hour and I probably understood about ten minutes worth of that conversation!

Another funny story took place at a Mexican restaurant in St. Louis that same year. My sweetheart Nicole and I were eating dinner when the waitress noticed my nametag and said, "So...your name is Collin, huh?"

"Yes, it is," I cordially responded.

This brought about a long conversation between the three of us about nametags and friendliness. As it turned out, "Wendy" had been wearing her permanent name tag every day for about eighteen years—I was so envious. To our surprise, this long conversation resulted in a free dessert for Nicole and me and a 90% tip for Wendy.

You gotta love fried ice cream.

Some Folk'll Never Wear a Nametag, and then Again Some Folk'll

Justin Diedrich

The first time I saw Scott wearing his nametag was at Denny's late one night about 2:30 AM. I noticed it on his shirt, but I didn't say anything. The next day he and I went thrift shopping and I saw that he was still wearing it. This time I said something.

I was speechless when he gave me his "Nametag Manifesto." It took him a while to explain his theory, but I guess he hadn't yet trimmed it down to "Skin and Bones."

I laughed aloud and tried to process all that he fit into his minute-long speech. Even so, I was hooked right away. So, on the drive back to finishing my freshman year at Case Western Reserve University, my suitcase was 500 nametags heavier!

The response was immediate and incredible. I've always had trouble with names, and I think it is because until I started wearing nametags, I never paid any real attention to them. But then I started really listening to people's names—and remembering them. I have found that to be one of the best things wearing a nametag has done for me.

I think initially my friends were amused, then intrigued. I have been spontaneous and eccentric all my life, so maybe wearing a nametag was a perfect fit for me...

In the first few months, the people I started to meet most often were the food service workers at school. I think cafeteria workers have always been great—whether you know their names or not. I also think many of them hated their jobs, and were eager to talk to any of us given the chance (or excuse).

The nametags were an instant conversation starter.

Unfortunately, the haste with which I usually found

myself running to class often resulted in sloppy handwriting. I *tried* to be careful when I wrote my name, but I usually ended up doing it in a hurry as I ran out the door, or as I sat down at my 9:30 class. This wasn't normally a problem except that "Justin," a name that may appear ambiguous at first glance, was often misinterpreted.

This brings me to Kim. She makes awesome pasta every lunch at my cafeteria, but she has called me Jason for the last eight months. The funny thing is that I watch her eyes glance at my nametag every time. Once she caught herself and apologized profusely, but promptly forgot the next day.

So what do you do when someone calls you the wrong name day in and day out?

Nothing. I wanted to correct her, but I just figured that deep down she really knew who I was. Well, maybe. But either way I smiled every time and said, "Hey, Kim, how ya doin'?"

One of my favorite jokes to play is to hide nametags at people's houses, in cars, in beds, even under trash cans. I don't like to throw them away, so I'd rather hide them to be found at a later date. Most of them are in my own house—there must be a hundred of them stashed in odd places. I even put one in Scott's car, and he didn't notice until a week had gone by! This is a great way to spread the message about friendliness, even if I'm not around. It's also a great way to drive people crazy!

However, the funniest story happened while visiting my girlfriend in Pittsburgh in May 2001. Niki's family was going to be meeting me for the first time, and I was very excited. We all got along really well, and everyone loved the nametag that I wore so religiously. Her grandparents especially loved the idea.

I returned to visit her family later that summer. We

were going to their family picnic at her grandparents' house, and I was a bit anxious because she had such a huge family, and there would be a score of new faces there.

When we arrived at the picnic there was an uproar—everyone there was wearing a nametag! They all put on nametags to make it easier on me! It was so much fun, and a great way to meet everyone in her family. How Amazing!

Collin Diedrich, Justin Diedrich, and I during Thanksgiving 2000 in St. Louis

HELLO, my name is Scott

Chapter 9

....

Worst Episode Ever

A positive attitude may not solve all your problems, but it will annoy enough people to make it worth the effort. — Herm Albright

As altruistic and constructive as theory may sound, I can't say that my nametag hasn't gotten me into a little bit of mischief over the years. I have dedicated the following chapter to a variety of stories, accidents, jokes and strange contexts in which I have found myself thanks to that little red and blue sticker.

As pointed out in earlier chapters, one of the most common responses to the nametag is, "Did you just come from work?" This is very logical and is probably what I would think if I saw someone walking around with a nametag.

Once again, for those who know me well, I'm the kind of person who likes to jokingly mess with strangers and do bogus role-playing and bullshitting with anyone just for fun. Of course, I never thought this would land me a job at a clothing store.

I went into American Eagle one day during the summer before my senior year. I was going there to visit my friend Pete who was managing the store at the time. He was dealing with customers, so I busied myself with the cabana flower shirt rack. About a minute later, a lady of roughly sixty-five years approached me and said, "Excuse me, Scott, but are you sold out of those flower shirts? I wanted to get one for my grandson."

Having just spent a short time looking at the shirts she was referring to, I just couldn't help getting sucked into this situation.

"Oh, sure, they're right over here," I said as I noticed red, green and blue color varieties of the same shirt. "Which color and size do you need?"

"I need a large blue one, please."

So I reached to the top rack and found the size she needed and said, "Take that up to the desk and Pete will check you out whenever you're ready, and thanks for shopping American Eagle."

I never did receive any commission for that sale.

That wasn't the only time I posed as an employee because of a false inference from my nametag.

I was typing a paper at one of the computer labs at school one day when I felt the need to make a phone call. So, I went to the Lab Consultant desk to use the campus phone. I sat there trying to remember someone's number when a student who appeared to be a freshman (they stand out like lightning bugs at midnight), approached me with a puzzled look on her face. I looked up at her, and before I could say anything, she said, "Hey, Scott, I think the printer is out of toner or something."

Now there was a situation that could get me into trouble if I handled it poorly, which I did.

"Oh, well, let's take a look at it then," I said with knowledgeable confidence.

I walked over to the printer and looked closely. It said, "Toner Low."

Shit.

I have no idea how to change the toner on a laser printer. Hmm. So I opened up the drawer that held the paper and checked that. Yep, plenty of paper. I guess that's not the problem. Yeah, that would be too easy.

So I opened the main panel to look for the toner cartridge and saw it blinking. This was a good sign. Thank God!

Worst Episode Ever

All I had to do was remove this cartridge and load in another one. That's what I would be saying if I weren't totally worthless when it came to computers.

I looked at the puzzled first year student and told her, "Let me call my supervisor and get another cartridge." I went over to the Lab Consultant desk again and picked up the phone. I called 523-9094, which was my home phone number at the time. My machine picked up and I said, "Yeah, this is Scott from Laws Computer Lab Room 11. I'm going to need a new ink cartridge for the...uh...Cannon Laser 2300...o.k., thanks." I had no idea if the damn printer was even Cannon, much less a 2300, but this worried girl had no idea.

"They're bringing it right down."

"Great, thanks."

She went back to her terminal to set up her print again, and I grabbed my bag, signed off the network and got the hell out of there.

However, probably the stupidest thing I've ever done while wearing a nametag was during the summer of 2000 in St. Louis. My friends and I regularly frequented a local bar and grill throughout our younger years called the Sports Page. We often went there to watch Blues, Cardinals, and Rams games on their big screens while enjoying great chicken wings and a friendly atmosphere. Unfortunately, while many of my friends had turned twenty-one, or had a driver's license that fraudulently said so, I was still under the legal drinking age. Even though my beverage of choice was and always has been scotch and soda minus the scotch, I still wanted to get into the bar and needed to find some form of alternate identification to do so.

My brother is almost eighteen months my senior, so

his old driver's license and our fairly noticeable resemblance turned out to be my ticket to fun. I obtained his license and would begin using it to pass as Steve Ginsberg for a few months, which was around the same time I began wearing my nametag—October 2000.

Despite our differences in eye color and height, there never seemed to be any problems getting into bars. So, one night over my holiday break in St. Louis, my friends Drew, Dan, Rob, and I went to the Sports Page to shoot some pool and enjoy a few pitchers. Since I was using a fake, I was to go third in line at the door. This is a common practice among underage drinkers who surround themselves with those who have legal forms of ID to "candy coat" the line at the door.

"Can I see some ID, please?" asked the bouncer.

"Here ya go," I said smoothly as I passed him my brother's license.

"So, *Scott*, What's with the nametag on your shirt?"

Oh, crap.

Dan and Rob looked back at me and shook their heads. Drew started laughing and walking the other way.

I was very close to thinking of some ridiculous explanation about a psychology experiment for my master's degree that would cover my mistake, but I just couldn't go through with it.

So, I lost it.

I busted out laughing right in the bouncer's face. I don't think he thought it was funny at all. I based this hypothesis on the dead-pan scowl on his face. To avoid further embarrassment I just hung my head low, didn't say a word, and walked back to my car.

Worst Episode Ever

To tell the absolute truth, I'll be the first person to poke fun at myself for wearing this damn thing, especially when I can use the immense recognition of it as a useful catalyst for a good joke. This self-mocking practice was put to use most effectively when my family visited me at college.

Long since aware of the tremendous effectiveness of the nametag, my parents suggested that they sport similar tags when visiting one weekend in March 2002. Grabbing a small handful of blank tags from my stack of thousands, I wrote with my same blue pen: "Scott's Mom" and "Scott's Dad."

As the three of us ventured around Oxford on Friday night, we experienced more laughs and greetings than we could possibly handle. My friends had never met my parents before, so without introduction they all became acquainted immediately.

"Hey! It's Scott's parents! All right!"
"Hey, Scott's Mom!"
"So, you must be Scott's dad, huh?"

Screams came from down the streets and across the bars. My parents were the coolest people on campus that night!

Later that same weekend my folks and I were shopping at a local gourmet foods market called Jungle Jim's. My dad and I perused the beef jerky aisle while my mom was nowhere to be found, but apparently she was more popular than we thought. An older man my dad didn't know approached him and said, "Hey, I know your wife!"

To make matters even more ridiculous, a few months later was graduation weekend. This brought participation from more members of my family. My grandparents, brother, and girlfriend all wore nametags bearing their relation to me:

> Scott's Grandpa
> Scott's Grandma
> Scott's Brother
> Scott's (as in "Property Of")

These new additions to my nametag posse elicited some memorable comments such as:

> "Hey, there's Scott's family!"
> "Hey, Scott, I think I just met your brother down the street!"
> "Are these your grandparents?"
> "Looks like you got the whole family doing it, huh?"

"At one point during our weekend visit, someone walked up to me and said, 'Hey, I'm a huge fan of your son!'"— Scott's Mom

"We got to see first hand the positive effects of nametag wearing—and all we had to do was walk into town, slap on our nametags, and the fun began! I think we stopped and spoke to every student and their family who was in town that weekend."— Scott's Dad

"First of all, there were at least fifty people who smiled at me and said, 'Hey, Scott's Grandpa.' But the funniest part of the weekend was when my nametag fell off my shirt and got stuck on the neighbor's dog, and everyone started to call the dog 'Scott's Grandpa.'"—Scott's Grandpa

Worst Episode Ever

(I must admit the obvious contradiction of this story to my altruistic theory of wearing a nametag. Giving my family nametags that merely read their relation to "Scott," as opposed to their true identity fuels my ego and doesn't necessarily work the same way to make people friendlier as the manner in which my nametag is normally worn. But hey, it's a funny story and life's full of inconsistency.)

Trying not to look too embarrassed, my parents give nametags a try.

Another great way to exploit the recognition of my nametag has been with the help of a Miami University late night favorite called Bagel and Deli. This hole in the wall has always been synonymous with great, eclectic food combined with a fun and crazy environment. Remaining open until the wee hours of the morning, the sandwich shop allows students to grab a late night snack to satisfy their hunger at the end of their uptown adventures.

Anyone who has had the pleasure of eating there will

tell you how difficult it is to order. In addition to a nightly packed crowd of drunken college students, each bagel sandwich has its respective sign on the wall depicting its ingredients, of which there are several dozen. Many of the bagels were created by Miami students themselves, with ingredients ranging from hummus to cream cheese to bell peppers.

After eating there for over a year, I decided to take a stab at creating my own bagel. Being such a big fan of spicy foods, I figured I would invent something a little zesty. Something that'd make you sweat. Combining roast beef and cheddar on a garlic bagel was not enough, so I added a big-ass pile of cayenne pepper. That was the final touch. My creation was done—the Scotty G bagel.

Nobody bought one for six months.

So, I began purchasing a Scotty G Bagel about once a week, just to make sure the sign wasn't taken down for lack of sales. Eventually some people tried it, although the popularity of this fire starter wasn't exactly catching on.

On the other hand, something else did catch on. The bagel was created in the spring of 2000, but I didn't start wearing my nametag until later that fall. Once I began sporting my daily label, the reactions from some of the Bagel and Deli employees began to accumulate. I immediately made friends with the owners, Gary and Ned, as well as most of the employees. Finally they started to put together the pieces that "Scotty G" was also "Scott with the nametag."

After a few months of getting acquainted with the store and its employees, my ordering process began to diminish

Worst Episode Ever

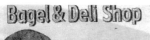

Bagel Of The Week

This week Bagel & Deli would like to honor a very special regular customer. One of the most memorable customers in Bagel & Deli history.

Scotty began frequenting the Bagel shop a few years ago when he first arrived on campus as a freshman. Quickly introduced to the employees through the large name tag that will always shine on any shirt he wears, Scotty has respectably earned his place in Bagel & Deli history with the "Scotty G. Bagel."

Scotty decided to start with his favorite breath mint, the garlic bagel. Then you add a large pile of dark brown roast beef, smothered in smoked cheddar cheese and lit with a big ass pile of cayenne pepper. Ah, but make sure Nancy makes it. She has an agreement with Scotty to add her special touch with the steamer to get it just right.

Scotty almost lost his fame with his creation since it was so close to the well-known "Hungry Heifer." But, they found a soft spot for their friend when he put a heart-warming note on the back of his sign.

Thanks to our good friend Scotty and the sensitive employees, all of you looking for some late night activity can rest assured that the girls will come running to taste your sweet breath after you finish shoving every last bit of this mouth-watering bagel down your throat. Just be sure to wash it down with a nice warm Natty Light. Mmm...tasty.

compiled by Maria Casey

This article from *The High Street Journal* for February 7, 2002, describes my culinary claim to fame.

The bagel. The man. The legend.

Employees of Bagel & Deli follow the trend of nametags.

quickly. I would usually walk in and greet whoever was working, to which they would ask if I wanted my bagel. I always did. By the end of my senior year, I didn't even have to ask. I walked in and they knew what I wanted right away.

This may not seem like a big deal, but anyone who has been to Bagel and Deli at 2:30 on Saturday morning after a long night can empathize. You literally cannot move in the store. It's not exactly the biggest place in Oxford, yet everyone crams into its friendly confines to eat the best steamed bagel sandwiches in the Midwest.

One Thursday night I walked into Bagel and Deli and noticed that one of the employees was wearing a nametag. I was a bit confused, until I approached the counter and saw all the employees look over to me—it turned out that particular night was "Nametag Thursday!"

Worst Episode Ever

As tradition would have it, one of the infamous antics of Bagel and Deli is their Thursday "Theme Nights." According to Gary, one of the managers, they try something different each week. In the past, Gary says they have done such crazy stunts as "sun glasses night," "hat night," and, of course, "no shirt night."

"Hey, Scott, we're all wearing nametags tonight too!" said my friend Nancy.

"Hey, this is great! Isn't it fun wearing nametags?!" screamed another employee.

Looking more closely at the nametags worn by the employees, I noticed none of their names were actually correct. Each person was mocking the idea of wearing a nametag with his or her own pseudonym. Some of my favorites were the slightly perverted and funny "Heywood Jablomi" and "May I. Gettawhat."

In the end, I was never certain whether or not their nametags were a coincidence or a complete mockery of my friendlier, more communicative society. I hope the latter.

Obviously, in all the years of my continuous nametag wearing, I've had a fair share of jokes played on me. Many have been minimal and only slightly amusing; however, my friend Andy decided to get me good once and for all.

He's a good guy. He rides around in a van and solves mysteries. This is the story according to him:

Andy Sweeney

I'm not sure what possessed me to do it. One night, a group of people from the radio station were hanging out. As usual, we began talking with Scott about his nametag, and I asked if I could wear one of his spare nametags because I knew that he always carried a few extras in his wallet. To make that story short, I grabbed a pen and was able to enjoy the evening as "Steve," which is not even my real name, but it was still fun to have people come up to me and say, "What's up, Steve?"

Several days later when I was preparing for the Red Brick Rasta, which is a huge street party in Oxford, I decided to wear a nametag yet again, but could not decide on a suitable name. After debating Steve, Seth, Vanessa and Vicki, the perfect name hit me: I would be Scott for the evening. What a great way to play a joke on him! My brother and girlfriend also decided to be Scott. So I wrote Scott on a 100 pack of nametags and went uptown. My goal was to saturate the area with pseudo-Scotts, as a tribute to the trendsetter himself. Friends from the radio station dropped their real names and became Scott. Friends I had not seen in years became Scott. Strangers I didn't even know were willing to undertake the false identity as Scott. Also, the lead singer of the performing band that night, whose name ironically enough was Scott, proudly sported a nametag for the duration of his performance. However, the funniest part was when two good-humored officers from the Oxford police department became Scott.

High Street became a mecca for people wearing Scott nametags. It was amazing. However, it was not nearly as amazing as the reaction from strangers. People came out of the woodwork to inform me that I was not the real Scott. Reactions ranged from drunken amused comments of "Hey, you're not Scott," to quietly upset accusations of "Hey, you're not Scott."

I have always said that Scott is a person who knows a lot of people, but I had no idea until that night—I guess wearing a nametag truly is a great way to make new friends. I think I met twenty new people that night, even though my identity was wrong. Playing that joke on Scott was great fun. His face was priceless when he showed up late and saw all the people with his name on their shirts. I will always remember the night that Oxford was overrun with a hundred Scotts.

Andy Sweeney and the members of the Oxford Police Department—
Officer Scott and Officer Scott

HELLO, my name is Scott

I have now survived close to 800 days without taking the nametag off. I have made a myriad of strangers and acquaintances friendlier and more sociable than they would have been otherwise. I have invited thousands of people to join me on my front porch in friendly interactions; most invitations have resulted in warm smiles and new relationships. Note the key word in that last sentence: "most."

It's not easy to admit, but I can imagine that at some point while reading this book, you've probably said to yourself, "This guy *has* to get his ass kicked *all* the time."

Well, not all the time…

In November 2001 I found myself walking alone past a bar called Attractions on a cool, Oxford night. As usual, a stranger leaning up against the outside window that was waiting in line to get into the bar yelled, "Hey, Scott!"

"Hey, man, what's goin' on?" I returned to the cowboy hat-clad fellow.

"I was wondering," he asked, while his breath screamed Jack Daniels, "Do you have a pen?"

"Oh…no, sorry, man, I don't have one on me."

"Oh. Well, I was going to say, if you did have a pen, I was going to write 'D-Bag' on your nametag."

I smiled and laughed along with him as he and his friend ridiculed me as if there was some type of inside joke between them that I didn't get. He was being a wise guy, but due to his size, facial hair and blood alcohol level, I didn't start anything. I just let him have his drunken fun so he could go home happy that night with the satisfaction that he cleverly referred to me as a feminine hygiene product. Good for him.

Worst Episode Ever

"Well, sorry, I can't help you out man."

He continued to smile as I shrugged my shoulders and began to step away. It was at this point that I made a crucial mistake. I didn't want to start a rumble or anything; I just felt the slightest bit of sarcasm towards tough guy #1 was in order to reciprocate the same courtesy with which I was treated.

"That stands for 'douche bag,' right? Just checking," I said.

Oh, boy, was that the wrong thing to say.

Forty-three seconds later, I was approached by this dude's friend (tough guy #2) to whom I had said nothing. He came up to me and said, "Hey, Scott, are you talking shit to my friend?"

"No man, he came up to me. I just told him I didn't have a pen."

"No...I think you were talking shit to him. I mean, do we have a problem here? Because I don't think we need to have a problem here."

Now it was grossly obvious these two guys had been sharing the same bottle.

"Look, buddy, I don't want to start any trouble. I didn't mean to offend anybody and I'm sorry if your friend thinks I am talking shit, but I'm telling you the truth. I'm sorry, man."

Pointing to my plastic glass of ice water, tough guy #2 said, "No, *Scott*, I don't think you are sorry. You're not sorry. You've been drinking and you're *not* sorry."

So I explained to this contentious gentleman that my friends and I were leaving anyway, and there would not be a problem. "Fine, whatever," he said.

I walked back over to my group of friends standing around, which is a common weekend activity in Oxford. I explained to them that some guys were being drunken idiots, and that there was nothing to worry about. And by *nothing* to worry about I mean the *rearranging of my face* to worry about. But further oddness was to follow.

Tough guy #2 came up to me yet again with another friend of his, whom I will refer to as "another really big guy who was going to kick my ass." He towered over me at roughly 6' 5" and outweighed me quite substantially at no less than 240 pounds, 97% of which appeared to be steel.

"Hi, Scott," he said with a handsome smile, "I'm Kevin. It's nice to meet you. Do we have a problem here?"

"Uh…no…there's no problem here, we just had a mis-communication and me and my friends are heading out for the night, so everything's cool."

"Well, good, I'm glad there's no problem."

Who the hell was this guy? Why was he so nice and his friends so stupid? I wasn't even scared anymore—this was the calmest, most sincere and efficient conflict resolution I had ever seen! Hell, I wanted to be this guy's friend.

So then tough guy #2 said as he hid behind Kevin's back, "Yeah, because…y'know Scott…we can kick your ass if you want us to…"

"No, no, no…that's not necessary. We're ready to leave anyway, so you guys can go back inside, and there's no problem here. Sorry again."

"Yeah, that's right, Scott," said tough guy #2.

Sure, tough guy #2 will say anything now that he's got his goon with him. . . Punk.

So maybe I set myself up for that one. The funny thing about that whole situation is the irony that lay within:

while tough-guy #1-drunken-redneck-insult-stranger-to-prove-to-my-friends-how-large-my-penis-is wanted to humiliate me by calling out my name to bring me over so he could poke fun at my nametag, he was actually doing exactly what I wanted him to do. Now, I can't say he was necessarily being friendlier, but more socially interactive, yes. So tough guy #1 thought he was being clever and witty by making fun of me to my face, but he actually was stepping onto my front porch—even if he wanted to ram my face into it.

HELLO, my name is Scott

Chapter 10

· · · · · · · · · · · · · · · · · ·

The World is a Mirror

We cannot hold a torch
to light another's path without brightening our own.
—Ben Sweetland

In the end, whether people are saying hello to me, starting a conversation with me, playing a joke on me, or talking about me, they are all being friendlier and more sociable in some way. These interactions have more than sufficiently satisfied my original objective for wearing a nametag. However, in the long run I have serendipitously become aware of several positive changes that unexpectedly occurred in my own life.

I am often asked if I am good at remembering people's names. Truthfully, I have always been just as forgetful as any other person. Once the first few months of wearing a nametag had gone by I met more people per week than ever before in my life—the only problem was that these people would never forget my name. On the other hand, I had to remember dozens of new people's names just as quickly as they knew mine. This was a lot harder for me than it was for them.

In fact, it was damn near impossible.

After a few months I came to the decision that my remembering people's names was vital. I thought it would be somewhat ironic and hypocritical if I couldn't remember the names of all the people I met! Many times I found myself in situations where, just like any other person, my memory failed me and I couldn't recall a single name! Some people found it irritating and contradictory that I couldn't remember their names. This destroyed my credibility and they made sure to point that out to me.

My tactic for remembering names has always been to repeat the name in my head when that person looks away, coughs, talks to someone else, or takes a break from talking to me. To say someone's name in my head only takes me a split second anyway, so I very rarely miss any important part of the dialogue.

This method usually works, but like any name-remembering trick, it fails occasionally—especially since I meet so many people. I suppose the only reason I have become super skilled at remembering people's names is because practice makes perfect. I meet so many people so often that I really have no choice but to remember their names. Just like any person who loses face when a name is forgotten, I do not want to look like an idiot—and I would probably look like the biggest idiot of all. After all, forgetting the names of dozens of people would be *a higher cost* to a man who has given his name out to everyone at *no cost*.

So, yes, I have forgotten names just like everyone else. No doubt there will never be a universal method for remembering names, unless we all wear nametags or something—but who the hell would ever want to do that?

Interestingly enough, wearing a nametag for so long has also increased my mindfulness and appreciation for other people's nametags. This has been a fascinating discovery.

There are already millions of people who wear nametags every day in their places of business. However, I never realized the attention and utilization those nametags fail to receive, yet rightly deserve.

Take purchasing groceries. Traditionally, when the

The World is a Mirror

clerk would hand me the receipt, thank me and tell me to have a nice day, I would say back to him, "Thanks, you too."

That is until I started wearing a nametag.

But since people obviously love to hear their own name more than any other word, and their names are right in front of my face anyway, I discovered that I now take advantage of the *free offering* of employees' names and use them whenever I talk to them.

Understandably, I would usually use this information provided to me by nametags when I *needed to get their attention*, but that would be the only scenario in which it was used. I now see nametags worn by employees, or anyone for that matter, as golden opportunities to use a stranger's name for no reason other than being friendlier and making them feel appreciated.

My lack of recognition for these brilliant smile creators known as nametags was first brought to my attention when I was buying groceries one afternoon. I had already been wearing my nametag for a few months, so I was recently attuned to the importance that names possessed.

After I got my bag and the clerk handed me my change, she said, "Thanks for shopping at Kroger."

I replied, "You're welcome, Sharon."

She glared at me curiously for a moment and slightly tilted her head. She then began to smile, then she chuckled, and I smiled back.

"Have a good day, *Scott*."

Apparently Sharon was not used to customers using her nametag as a tool for friendly conversation. In fact, I would guess the last time someone took advantage of her nametag for introductory purposes was when she first became an employee at Kroger.

HELLO, my name is Scott

This story sparked a trend in my conduct that I have continued to this day: I always use people's names when they are freely given to me by nametags. The reason it has become so important to me is because I *know* how great it feels when strangers use my name and make the effort to be friendlier. So I try to take advantage of that situation to help reciprocate the same joy and warmth that is extended to me every day.

Another behavior that has developed over the years of wearing a nametag has been my increased willingness to stand out among the crowd. Frankly, I've always been a non-conformist and very willing to be different. If you've ever seen some of the clothes I wear you probably know what I'm talking about. But since October 2000 I have become accustomed to the fact that wherever I go, people are going to stare at me. Whenever I walk into a room, people are probably going to talk about my nametag to the person next to them. So I have accepted the idea that I stand out in every situation and will always look slightly different from the person in front of me.

Big deal.

Actually it used to be a big deal. The first few months of wearing a nametag were not easy. Knowing that people were gawking and talking about the nametag was pretty uncomfortable for me.

And then there were my friends. Oh, how they hated it. Not only did strangers stare at me, but they stared at them, too. My brother even ripped it off my shirt four times in one night because he was so uncomfortable with it! Good thing I had all those spares in my wallet!

I must say it took a while to get used to that kind of stuff. But around the same time I discovered the amazing effects the nametag had on *other* people, I also discovered the **TYS Factor**, which stands for "Throw Yourself into the Sea."

I found out that essentially what I undergo when I wear a nametag is this process of throwing myself into the sea—the *sea* being the world and the *throwing* being the offering of my identity to that world.

At first, this process made me uncomfortable. I could even feel the people around me pondering about the oddness of a man wearing a nametag all the time. It was discomforting, and to say the least, *embarrassing*. No wonder so many people would never want to wear a nametag!

Keeping in mind the true goal of wearing a nametag, I did my best to shake that discomfort and tried hard to keep focused on my philosophies of friendliness and familiarity. Gradually it became easier to ignore. After a while I got used to standing out and eventually stopped thinking about it all together.

In essence, TYS served as my *variable of discomfort reduction*. I learned that the more often it was used, or the more frequently I threw myself into the sea, the lower my ultimate discomfort became.

In short, the more often I threw myself into the sea, the less often the waves affected me.

TYS had a huge impact on me. Every new day of wearing a nametag, or every new day of throwing myself into the sea brought about more exposure to people wondering why the nametag was there. I eventually stopped caring what people were saying and thinking behind my back and went on with my business.

And, as the uneasiness I felt about walking around every day with a nametag diminished, other discomforts decreased as well. I have now become considerably less fearful in social situations because I am so used to ignoring criticism anyway. I can walk into any room or any bar with almost any group of people and feel perfectly at ease.

Why?

Because I just don't care. I don't mean that in an apathetic or arrogant way. I just don't care. People can say what they want, but the bottom line is that I have become used to it, and it no longer affects me. Two years ago I may have felt strange as the only person walking into a room wearing a nametag, but not any more.

Finally, wearing a nametag has made me a happier person. Of all the improvements to my character that resulted from wearing my nametag, increased happiness has been the most apparent. Much like remembering/using names and being willing to stand out, having a positive and happy personality is something that I have always considered a part of my life, even before wearing a nametag. Ask any person who's known me for a few years; I've always been a happy guy! However, my happiness has been accentuated and improved as a result of wearing a nametag for several reasons.

One Thursday morning I was walking to work in a really crappy mood. It was cold outside, my nose was stuffed up, and I was stressed out about a few things. Just before entering the building I was greeted by an older man who appeared to be a professor.

"Morning, Scott!" he said in a cheerful voice.

"Good morning, how are you?"

"I'm doing fine, thanks. So…do you have a convention or something to attend today?"

"No, I always wear this nametag. It makes people friendlier and more sociable."

The World is a Mirror

"Really? You *always* wear it?"

"Yeah, it's a great way to make people more willing to communicate and also helps them remember my name so they don't feel as bad."

"Wow! What a great idea. You must be a psychology student or something."

"No, I just do this for fun and to help other people."

"Interesting."

At that moment, I realized I was no longer in a bad mood. I was still cold. I still had hours of work to do. And I still couldn't breathe through my nose. But on the other hand I just had a conversation with a complete stranger who was very friendly to me. It really cheered me up.

Conversations with strangers just like that one have been instrumental in making me a happier person. And, no matter how good or bad my mood, it always continues to get better over the course of the day. No, not because I get attention all the time, but because I meet and talk with new people every day who would have otherwise not said a single word.

I also smile a lot more often. Smiling has become very important to me since I have started wearing a nametag because I use it as a means through which I express my desire to make people friendlier. In short: smiling complements wearing a nametag.

The importance of smiling was explained best to me when I read a piece called "The Value of a Smile" in *How to Win Friends and Influence People* by Dale Carnegie.

"A smile costs nothing but creates much. It enriches those who receive without impoverishing those who give. It happens in a flash and the meaning of it sometimes lasts forever. None are so rich they can get along without and none so poor but are richer for its benefits. It creates happiness in the home, fosters good will in a business and is the countersign of friends. It is rest to the weary, daylight to the discouraged, sunshine to the sad and nature's best antidote for trouble. Yet, it cannot be bought, begged, borrowed or stolen, for it is something that is no earthly good to anyone until it is given away."

In the past two years, I have probably said hello to over two thousand random strangers who saw my nametag and then used it to initiate their greeting. And, minus a few people who wanted to kick my ass, I have never neglected to answer back to someone with a pleasant "hello," "what's up?" or "how are ya?" More importantly, I have never neglected to answer back but with a big, toothy grin on my face.

Finally, my happiness has escalated because I have realized that wearing a nametag is a courteous, free offering of my name—and it often serves as an act of kindness. It reminds people who I am. It gives their brains a rest and makes them more comfortable. I can't even begin to count how many people have actually thanked me for wearing a nametag because they had trouble remembering who I was. This made me realize that wearing a nametag stimulated a sigh of relief for which many people were very appreciative. And, when people don't have to worry about remembering my name and feel less apprehensive, I have the gratifying feeling of service, albeit a small service.

Sir James M. Barrie once said, "Those who bring sunshine to the lives of others cannot keep it from themselves." Wearing a nametag has allowed me not to keep the sunshine

The World is a Mirror

from myself. When people remember my name, I remember theirs. When a stranger smiles at me, I smile back. When people appreciate and utilize my nametag, I appreciate and utilize their nametags. And, when somebody willingly offers their friendliness to me, I willingly offer my friendliness to them.

The world is truly a mirror!

HELLO, my name is Scott

Chapter 11

....

Take Care of the Inches and Forget about the Miles

If a window of opportunity appears, don't pull down the shade.
— *Thomas J. Peters*

So that's pretty much it.

That's the kind of stuff that happens to me every single day. Except for the ass kickings—those only happen about once a month.

To my surprise, I have found that people are actually a lot more willing to talk to me than I thought. In fact, they're a lot more willing to talk to me than *they* thought; they just don't realize it until they take advantage of the golden opportunity that is offered to them on my front porch.

You see, most people, unfortunately, do not recognize their desire and potential to be friendly, willing communicators. Since they are usually preoccupied by the apprehension of uncertainty and inapproachability, the opportunities to meet new people and to better relationships are often missed. But the bottom line is that most people *do* have a yearning to socialize with others and make new friends; they just need more opportunities (and less apprehension) to understand that desire.

So, therein lies the secret for making people friendlier and more sociable: **creating more opportunities for them to do so.**

I think people *will consider* stepping onto someone's front porch if that porch seems approachable. In point of fact, that was the original motivation behind the front porch over 100 years ago—approachability. People wanted others to come to their house to talk and get to know each other and ultimately build a community of closely knit friends; it was just a heck of a lot easier with such a welcoming gesture.

Likewise, the simple act of wearing a nametag is one of a dozen ways to do the exact same thing on a smaller scale! By immediately familiarizing people with who I am, I become more approachable to them because I have lowered their uncertainty and communication apprehension. At this point, they feel significantly more comfortable talking to me and therefore take advantage of my nametag as an opportunity to begin or better our relationship. Most importantly, in the end they have stimulated their underestimated willingness to be friendlier.

In fact, wearing a nametag isn't even necessary for building more front porches to encourage people to be friendlier—that's just one way to do it! As I explained in the beginning of the book, my goal is not to convince people to wear nametags, but to illustrate my own simple method for creating a friendlier society in the hope that the readers will discover *their* own way, nametag or no nametag.

Now if someone does discover that their way to make people friendlier is to wear a nametag, that's great! In fact, for those brave souls who'd like to get a head start on the construction of their front porches, I have even thoughtfully included two blank nametags in the back of this book.

But the truth, my friends, is that one could easily use any number of congenial actions on a daily basis to stimulate and enhance the level of our society's interpersonal communication! Things like smiling, making people laugh, starting conversations with strangers, remembering to use people's names, or simply saying hello to those who cross your path are all small, yet effective tools for voluntarily offering yourself for the purpose of bettering social interaction.

Take Care of the Inches and Forget about the Miles

Give it a try! I think you'll be pleasantly surprised with the number of friendly responses you get from people if you simply take that first step and extend yourself!

After all, why not go out on a limb—isn't that where the fruit is?

Acknowledgements

This book would not exist without the assistance, direction, time, and patience of my mentor and great friend, William Jenkins. He has been a guiding force in my life since I was sixteen, and I am forever grateful for his invaluable advice. Speaking of invaluable, my parents probably deserve to be thanked more than anyone. Words cannot possibly describe the gratitude and love I feel for them, and I am so lucky to have been raised by such amazing people who have loved me so much and have accepted the fact that I am a complete putz. I would also like to thank the entire Ginsberg family for all of their encouragement and unconditional love that has kept me strong over the years.

Parts of this book were contributed by many great friends whose words were vital to its success: Dr. Tom "Norb" Speh, Justin D. Ellis, Justin Diedrich, Collin Diedrich, and Andy "Capatin Fisto" Sweeney.

Organizational layout, editing and proofreading were graciously done by Lenora Hobbs, with additional patronizing and red penning by the great Tony "Red Leader" Cameron.

I would also like to thank Maco Tag and Label for making a fine quality product that has been and will always be my sole source for creating a friendlier society.

My Website, www.hellomynameisscott.com was created and managed by Aheadhosting under the direction of the great Chad Kouse.

Due to death threats received via email, I have been obligated to credit the following members of the Alpha Sigma Sigma fraternity, est. 2001: Dan O'Grady, John O'Grady, Aaron Farmer and John H. Board.

Special thanks to the following professors who actually made learning fun: Dr. David Rosenthal, Dr. Thomas Speh, Ellen Young, Dr. Thomas Boyd, Dr. Charles Crespy, Tom Humbach, Bond Benton, Holly Wilkin, Minet Schindeheutte, Gillian Oakenful, Dr. Chuck Crain, Dr. David Carr and Julio Videras.

Additional thanks to BookMasters, Miami University, Bagel and Deli, WMSR Redhawk Radio, Matt Groening, Kirk Lintern of Who's Your Daddy Records, Jerry Seinfeld, Will Ferrell, Bryan Fellows, Ekoostik Hookah, Skynyrd, Electric Solitude, Jackson Rohm, Adam Duritz, Mark Sandman, Chris Whitley, Ben Harper, George Carlin, and last but not least, the raisin guy.

Finally, thank you for taking the time to read my book.

Thank you for reading *HELLO, my name is Scott*!
If you are interested in purchasing more copies, please send
payment and this form to:

Front Porch Publishing
Scott Ginsberg
2109 NW Irving
#103
Portland OR 97210

Each copy is $12.95 plus shipping and handling of $2.00
per order. If you order 8 books or more, shipping is free!

Please pay by cash, check, or money order ONLY.

Include your shipping address below:

Name_____

Address_____

City_____ State_____ ZIP_____

Email_____

Phone_____

Where you bought this book_____

If you have any questions, please visit our Website at
www.hellomynameisscott.com
or email Scott at scott@hellomynameisscott.com